Amaranth

Amaranth

D.K.

VIDELICET

SAN FRANCISCO

Grateful acknowledgment is made to the editors of Videlicet for the collection of these poems in this first printed edition.

Videlicet Press

San Francisco, CA

Printed in the United States of America

Published in 2014 by Videlicet Press

ISBN-13: 978-0615943923

ISBN-10: 0615943926

for Her

eiv klhoronomian afqarton kai amianton kai
amaranton, tethrhmenhn en ouranoiv eiv umav

—*I Peter*

Immortal amarant, a flow'r which once
In Paradise, fast by the Tree of Life
Began to bloom, but soon for man's offence
To Heav'n removed where first it grew, there grows,
And flow'rs aloft shading the Fount of Life,
And where the river of bliss through midst of Heav'n
Rolls o'er Elysian flow'rs her amber stream;
With these that never fade the Spirits elect
Bind their resplendent locks inwreathed with beams.

—*Milton, Paradise Lost*

CONTENTS

Amaranth

CATHEDRAL SPIRES

Extended in solitude
        toward blind night,
Bone-white fingers
        reach for another's hand

DREAMS FROM GOLDEN HILL

I

Windows on burnt palms, dry beards hanging in the heat.
Desert wind, devoid of adornment, scatters sands
Like tea leaves in our cups,
Where we search for a glimpse of time's tracings.

What is it we would know?
What secrets in these hands we reach to learn?
To speed the shortness of breath.
                              Time, so short.

The blue jay's daily morning cry answers all
                              The world could know.
Clear voices, dried flowers, sifting varied scents.
                    Listen to the wind.

II

The wash of jet wake overhead, morning psalm,
With open hands, a welcome path into the world.
Sunlight golden on the sheets, somewhere
Between the embrace of dream and memory.

Time's trinity, turning into what is now.
Nostalgia floats in a clear glass bowl,
Its petals filling the room
                              With sweet perfume.

I would slow the sun and lie here, tracing
                                    Shadows of morning solitude,
Until each curve of her body and her face
                                    Was printed into time's moods.

MEMORY OF RIMINI

Think of spring,
The gray sky of Rimini,
Where we stopped that day
And walked together
Through the cobbled streets,
While the salt-sea mist
Drifted lightly cool
Across your face,
Frosting your hair like night dew;

You laughed and brushed
The wet strands from your eyes,
And I searched in their dark depths
As you smiled and talked
Of the day we walked in the rain
That first year in San Francisco.

Chilled, we stopped and sat in the piazza,
Waiting for our train,
Watching the old men smoking quietly
In their tweed coats and caps,
Amid the sounds of children playing,
And memories of San Francisco
Drifting through our silences.

LET ME EVEN NOW REMEMBER

Let me even now remember
The sound of your voice—
You, who have gone
To the realm of the departed,
Where lie those who are lost
Like the dead.

Let me even now remember
Your words, your face—
Faded now, shadowy,
Like an ancient Greek sculpture,
Scarred, yet still standing in its
Watery, Mediterranean grave.

AMARANTH

Had I known then
This bitterness of regret,
My daughter of winter,
Conceived in this season of spring,
I would never have let you go
Before you had breathed even once
The air upon this earth.
To be here now, five years old,
Made in her image,
A reminder
Of she who is gone.

But, perhaps,
It is better
That you never knew the pain and suffering
Of this life.
Taken in innocence,
Pure essence of love
Never given the chance to fade,
Bright in your bloom eternal
And timeless as the amaranth
You live within my heart.

Yet, still,
I would have you
Here with me now,
To teach you and watch you grow,

To hold you and protect you,
Together within this world,
This life then complete.
For I long for you now
Even more than I long for her.

THE THING ITSELF

I have lived in cities
Where the fog rolled nightly
Through the streets
Like the sweetest memories of youth
Slipping quietly along
The unmapped avenues of the mind,
Transforming ordinary streetlights
Into a halo of shimmering brilliance,
Alluring, like the body
Of a woman seen
Through the sheerness
Of a negligee.

All so romantic;
But would we not rather see plainly
The thing itself?
In a clarity unobscured
By the lens of imagination?
Can we not accept the blackbird
As merely a black bird?
A rose as no more, and no less,
Than a rose?

I have lived in cities
Where the fog rolled cold death over the land
Like the smooth hands of a minister
Administering a child's last rites,

And I know that what we call knowing
Resides in the mind
Like images of foreign cities
We might once have read about
Or seen on a postcard
Sent by a forgotten friend.

SHADOW AND LIGHT

All day the sun spun shadows
Across the world. And I,
Watching from the window,
Saw their movement in my mind,
Circling forward and then back
Yet all the while motionless.

And now, in night's nearness,
I understand the violence
Of that warring—which seemed
No more than simple play—and
The supremacy of darkness,
Which needs no light to live.

ORPHEUS

for H.D.

I

Have I lost you yet again?
You who brought this living world
To life,
You who roused these flowers
Into bloom:

O what bitter pain,
What cruelty is this?
What utter blackness
Have I now become?
O what have I done?

You, who lit the darkness
With your light,
You had returned
To taste this fragile air,

But for my lack of strength,
This weak and bitter rashness,
This blind impetuosity;
You, who should have breathed among the living;
I, who loved you, have slain you
In this second death.

II

Here, sunlight danced,
Golden against a sea of blue,
And green and red,
As the tulips bloom;
All blackened now
By one careless glance
That slaughtered beauty,
For this earth died with you;

Your hands,
Your face,
Your eyes,
Your lips;
Why must these poisoned eyes
Turn cold death upon you?

What falseness fueled that desire
To possess you utterly?
What light did make me blind?
What fire stoked this heart
That blackened this my soul?

What weakness made me turn
Away from light,
Toward darkness
Flowing upward

From its bed
Of lifeless ash,
Breathless silence,
Deep nothingness,
To hear you breathe farewell,
So black.

III

Dark cinders from below the earth,
Moss-stained darkness
Sweet with decay,
Swept up from the dead land,
Where withered lilacs lie;

All is covered,
All is crossed with death,
painted with blackness,
layer upon layer,
until no light shines through.

IV

Wet, dripping walls,
Tangled cavern
Of roots and dark sludge,
Rooted thickness,
Of life reaching downward,
Seeking;

Roots,
Driving down into the dead land,
Slim tendrils
Seeking sustenance,
Sucking life,
From death,
Above the earth;
If I could but descend again,
Return unto those depths,
To breathe life once more into you;
The roots tremble,
And the black;

To return or not, then, matters little;
A bed of soft lichen,
And the breathless air;
No longer is this loss.

V

So for this weakness,
This blind rashness,
I have lost you yet again,
Banished you from life
And so myself with you;
You, who reached up from the darkness
To feel again the warmth
Of light;

Your face must illuminate that world,
A deep red burning radiance
Of passion and defiance;

Your beauty could not die
For the tragic foolishness
Of man;
Such loss could not exist;
Such passion, such love, such life,
Though bound
By blackness
Still must burn;

Where you pass
In silence
Within those formless walls,
Beauty will be reborn,
The mirror of that blackness
That I carry
Upon this earth;
The dark longing of this face
That stains the earth
Where my sad sight falls.

VI

My song lies lifeless,
No longer have I words,

No music stirs within this heart;
Black as the depths
From which you rose,
And to which I've sent you back.

Blind, guilt-torn,
I would tear my eyes
For you;
Sight is nothing,
For I see only you,
Pale and lifeless,
Wrapped in the cold, white winding sheet.

VII

Bitter blame rests heavy
Upon this heart; broken
In despair and loss;
Forever to your love I pledge,
And spill this blood for you;

And in the bitterness
Of this loss;
Though dead upon this earth,
Doomed to wander,
Within this reminder that is life;
Already lost,
With you I linger
And will forever rest.

SONG OF ST. CECILIA

If I speak honestly—
If I speak plain truth—
Will you betray me?
If I reveal this song
That sings within my heart—
Will I lose you
To another?

Will I lose you
To one who is willing?

If I speak honestly?
Then you must know—
That I am given
To another—

Yet, still,
I would have you—
Though I fear,
I have lost you already.

Could you but hear that song
Within your heart,
Allow this love
To bring you peace—

If I speak honestly—
If I speak plain truth—
Could I hope, beyond hope,
That you will listen
And believe?

VALHALLA

What honor is this?
What use this immortality?

One man, merely,
Among a multitude
Of brave heroes, sad heroes—
Bound, all, to the cold
Confines of that hall—

What glory lies in this?
This endless fighting and feasting—
This abundance of meat and mead—

What honor is this?
What use this black reward?

O wish-maiden—
White-armed Valkyrie—
You, who have never tasted
The sweet joy of love—
How could you comprehend?

This pale affront to courage—
This, your dark proclamation
Of death—
Bears no such reward—

Better you rain down cold death—
That I might taste the glittering steel,

The fury of your shield and spear—
Than to embrace this faceless glory—
To abandon my one, my true, eternity—

What honor is this?
What use—

BONFIRE

Until the coals caught flame,
And the gathered driftwood
Unleashed bright burnings—
And a circle of dim faces emerged,
Seated around the fire pit
Like an ancient people—
Hunters, fishers, storytellers—
The flickering beginnings of civilization—

Until the snap of sparks
Jumped from the salt-stained wood,
And flames rose from the pit,
There was only darkness—
And the blind crunch of thick sand—
And the clotted redolence
Of seaweed and salt—
And the rhythmic beckon
Of the soughing sea—

I WALKED OUT INTO THE LIGHT

I walked out into the light
Where long shadowed fingers lay
Spread across the grass,

Bright stealthy blades
Beneath the branches of the magnolia tree
Grown now tall above the house,

Gnarled and twisted
Like an aged arthritic hand
That grips the yard in darkness,

But for the slivers of light
That scalpel through,
Deep lines like the scars

You studied before the mirror,
Turning away when I touched you
And said, "You're beautiful."

I walked out into the light
And remembered how you used to laugh
And play with Sarah,

Barefoot on the fresh green sod,
Learning to take that first step forward
Before the ivy grew its tangled web

Along the sagging fence,
A time when light still fell
Effortlessly and warm;

And now, married, a child
Of her own, in another sunlit land,
And a phone call at Christmas,

A letter now and then.
So far away, distant, changed,
Yet, still, so close.

I walked out into the light,
My hands time-twisted as the magnolia
Now, and remembered

How I used to hold you in the night
And feel the rhythm of your heart
Against my chest,

While we drifted
Silently together
Through the darkness.

EVENING STAR

You appeared to me
    like a dream
        in the night,

Suddenly there
    where before
        had been only darkness,

Brighter than
    the infinite
        lesser lights

Scattered dimly
    across the
        night-black sky,

I felt your presence,
    clear and brilliant,
        as our eyes met

Across that void.
    Now, captivated,
        I watch you glow,

Lovely, unattainable,
    and reach for you,
        already knowing

You cannot be there
  when morning comes
    and steals this dream away.

FIGS

If I dream
I love you
do I love you?

Could summer thunder-
showers bring relief
from this heat?

Bright sunlight
on the fig trees
ripens dark fruit—

Spring's delicate buds
bend now low
along the limbs—

To be torn
and tasted—
or, ignored,

To burst open
beneath this heat
and bleed down upon the earth—

But no,
love is nothing
like this—

Love comes
in a flash,
like the thunderstorm—

And rains down
with a desperate fury,
if but briefly.

SUMMER NIGHT

Tonight,
The heat beads and drips
Down the plastered walls
Of this empty room
Like the mournful liquid melody
Of Miles Davis on the radio.

While outside,
The streets lie silently lethargic,
And across the city
Windows open to the air,
Stirred only by the restless
Sweep of fans
That search like spotlights
Through the night
For fugitive relief.

BEYOND THE DARKNESS

Beyond the darkness of your eyes
I see,
Beyond my own sight's blindness,
A sense of recognition.

What lies within
Your silences?

Soon,
Summer's heat will soften,
The leaves begin to fall.

Through the darkness
Our eyes will touch
And fall, in wonder
Of worlds beyond the darkness
Where all is now silence, all.

TULIPS

Too brilliant,
Your soft, red petals.
Smooth and glossy
Like polished fingernails.

Your long, thin stalks,
Like the fragile glass stem
Supporting a goblet of cabernet.
Dainty between two fingertips,
While red painted lips
Drink your dark bloom.

Too brilliant,
Your bright red confidence.
That overripe heat
Melts you from within.

Like glowing glass,
Your petals curl and drip.
And your stem already
Begins to bend and droop,
Unable to support
Your beauty's blind weight.

ONE VOICE, ALONE

One voice, alone, I hear within this world.

Her whisper floats on the evening breeze,
Light fingers fanning the trees' dark leaves,

Like remembered tracings of her hands upon my face,
The warmth of her breath, the softness of her lips.

One voice, alone, I hear within this world.

Her laughter echoes in the gurgling sea,
The sweetest echo of that sweeter sound,

The tide that sweeps me back into her depths,
Then leaves me there to drown in silent seas.

The morning mist lies lingering like her sighs.
Her tears fall sadly in the weeping rain.

A plaintive chirp upon the windowsill
Calls out her name, and I wonder in its song,

"If I had loved her less, would her love
have lasted longer?" and listen for reply.

One voice, alone, I hear within this world.
I wake to feel the sunlight of her eyes,

But find only sadness in cloudy skies,
And know that though I held her closely once,

She is gone. Though I held her tightly, the sky
Turned around, and she is no longer mine.

For I did not have the strength to keep her,
And she is gone, and my love has left me.

No longer do I need to possess her,
Yet, to see her blue eyes, to hear her voice.

Already, she lies in another's arms, and
She is happy. She no longer needs me.

Yet, I would have her, if but for a moment.
Her whisper, her laughter, her anger, her

Pain. One look, alone, would heal my sorrow.
Why must memory always outlast love?

We pay love's price with long remembrances,
And so, I dream my days in thoughts of her.

after Neruda

31

DAYS OF 1991

I long to stop again at the Café Greco
On a warm afternoon in late October,
Linger once more at a sidewalk table, a glass
Of red wine, a game of backgammon, and live
Again, if but for a moment, in your voice.

And as the evening fog takes wing,
The first hint of winter in the salted air,
Walk along Columbus, hand in hand,
Watching the streetlights blink on, one by one,
And the red neon glow of cafes and restaurants.

Then ride together through the city streets,
The scent of October in the evening air,
Your arms tied tightly around my waist;
And outside your apartment, kiss you goodnight,
Your pale blue eyes, the taste of your lips.

And I long to climb the stairs to my studio,
Turn on the light, take a book from the shelf,
Sit down and read again for the first time
Of Yeats' red rose, before coming to know
What must be known to write those words.

SAN DIEGO SERENADE

— fall voices —

I

September rain
    drips lightly
        down the leaves
    soft and sweet
        in change of season
sorrow
    washing clean
summer's lonely light
        like the sudden
            first bright rustle
                of new love
such sudden joy
        comes tinged
            with strains
    of sadness
            lost
        yet found
            in the letting go

II

As darkness falls
     a rustling begins
        white jasmine petals
  opening before the night
and soon
     the air
  is full of your perfume
       rising
          like desire
     descending
  into dream

III

Dry as dust
  the desert
    winds blow
Santa Ana season
  clear as cactus dreams
      fired in the kiln
    of consciousness
  in this sleepy
     adobe-drawn town
dry and cool
    the night wind rises
      driving through the darkness
    like the distant howl
      of the coyote

IV

The October night breeze
                lifts the scent
of orange blossoms
        up to the window
where I sit writing
                these songs
and I glance up
        to a world
gone now stranger
                than dreams

V

Dark city
        drawn into a dream
strange as night
        and restless sleep
                of roads
        that lead to nowhere
but endlessly return
        to night
                and dreams
                        within the dream
What could it mean?
                What could it mean?

VI

Lie down
        beside me
in the Grant
        Park grass
and turn your eyes
        up toward the sky
and let the light
        wash over your face
and tell me
        what you see

VII

Blood of the mother
                Blood of the daughter
  blood of life
        and death
bright red blessing
  drips from the wound
                where life begins
Blood of the son
                Blood of the father
  stains the earth
        and the evening sky
                dropping like petals
                        into the night

36

VIII

Farewell
to all the flowers
that fled
their beauty
before our lips
Farewell
to all the daisies
of those days
and roses
of those nights
Farewell
to all the flowers

IX

Save a kiss for me
sweet sister midnight
and the whisper
of your secrets
glittering starlight
What lies beyond
the clouds
that darken
your soft brows?
Could it be
a place
of pure peace?
tranquility

X

A bright December sunset
             over Ballast Point
                      from the rocks
             along the boardwalk
                   of the beach in Coronado
 land's end
              dark Pacific
                       rim of the Western World
light conducting an elemental adagio
          in modalities of earth, air,
                      fire and water
                 a San Diego serenade
                          youth's final farewell
   voice of beauty
                      mystery
           for which
                we have no words
                     merely the sense
 of something sacred
                    something subtle
                 and fleeting
                             beyond
    the bounds of language

ENVOI

My spirit lives
        in the evening light,
Think of me
        now and then